Unbelievable Pictures and Facts About Northern Lights

By: Olivia Greenwood

Introduction

The Northern Lights are a beautiful masterpiece that can be seen in the sky. People travel from far and wide to see these lights. Today we will be learning all about the Northern Lights.

Why do people prefer these lights?

People prefer the Northern lights for a couple of different reasons, one of these reasons is that these lights are more accessible and appear more often.

Which lights do people prefer the Northern or the Southern?

The majority of people prefer the Northern lights over the Southern lights.

Are there any myths about the dancing lights?

There are plenty of myths about these lights. Some people actually think that they are spirits dancing.

Are all the good viewing areas accessible?

Unfortunately, there are many viewing areas that are not accessible to humans, as they are dangerous areas and not safe for viewing purposes.

Where are the greatest chances of seeing the lights?

There are a few places which give you the best chance possible of seeing the lights, these places include Alaska, Northern Canada, Iceland, and Norway.

Is it considered to be one of the 7 wonders?

Once again the answer is a big yes, as they are considered to be a part of the seven natural wonders of the world.

Are the Auroras very high up?

The answer is a big yes they are very high up.

What ways do the lights appear?

The lights actually appear in many different ways, they never will appear in exactly the same way. Each and every single occurrence is totally unique.

Do the lights ever appear to be changing shape?

Many times it may look like the lights are changing shape, as they appear in many different forms and patterns.

Do these lights only happen on earth?

It may be very interesting for you to learn that these lights also happen on other planets, not just here on earth.

Should humans be scared of the lights?

The good news is that humans should not be scared of the lights at all, because it is so high up it can't hurt us at all.

Can you see the Northern Lights anytime during the year?

You can see the lights anytime during the year, however, there are months when they are more visible than others.

Are the Southern lights very visible?

The truth is that the Southern Lights are nowhere near as visible as the Northern Lights.

Where are the lights the most visible?

One of the places where the lights are the most visible is a place called Fairbanks which is situated near the North Pole.

Do the lights last for a long time or not?

If you are lucky enough to catch the Northern Lights, you need to know that they only last for around 15-30 minutes at a time.

Which colors are the lights?

The lights are all different colors, they can be pink, yellow, green, blue, violet, red and combinations of different colors.

Are the Northern Lights predictable or not?

Unfortunately, the Northern Lights are not predictable and this makes it much harder for everyone.

What was the name of the person who discovered the Northern Lights?

The name of the man who first discovered the lights was Pierre Gassendi who was an astronomer.

Is there another name for the Southern Lights?

The name "Aurora" comes from Latin, meaning sunrise. In mythology, Aurora was the Roman goddess of dawn.

What is another name for the Northern Lights?

It may be useful for you to learn that the lights are also called Aurora borealis.

Printed in Great Britain
by Amazon